Ollie's Day Out

A Play by Carl Nelson

ISBN-10: 069233047X
ISBN-13: 978-0692330470

ii

DEDICATION

To the memory of Irv Zimmer

Plays by Carl Nelson:
Into the Wild Blue Yonder
Personal Growth Through Copier Sales
Ollie's Day Out

Essays by Carl Nelson:
The Audience is a Mob

Poetry by Carl Nelson:
A Poet's Past Lives
Shoving My Way Into the Conversation

All are currently available through Amazon books.

CONTENTS

ACKNOWLEDGMENTS

Ollie's Day Out was developed through readings at the Seattle Playwrights Studio at ArtsWest in West Seattle and through a staged reading in their 2008 Showcase. Ollie's Day Out was first produced as part of the Seattle Stone Soup Theater's Outside the Box Short Play Festival in 2008, where it won first prize.. Roi-Martin Brown Directed. Jorj Savage played Ollie. Angela Redman played Niki. Aaron Heinzen played Paul

OLLIE'S DAY OUT

CHARACTERS:

OLLIE BROWNSTONE: male, 84
NIKI SYLVESTER: woman, mid-twenties
PAUL RASMUSSEN: male, mid-twenties

OLLIE'S DAY OUT

SCENE 1

"My neighbor puts a piece of pineapple on his tongue like a sacrament,
sucks the juice out of it, chews it up, then turns
his head slow like a cloud and says *I can love anybody I feel like loving.*
And I say *that's ridiculous.*
And he says *what's ridiculous is that you don't. ….*"
- Matthew Dickman, Poet

SETTING: Stools are arranged facing the audience. It's "Fitzgerald's", a
hotel bar in the late-afternoon decorated for the Christmas holidays. The
patrons sit facing out into the audience as if into a bar mirror. NIKI, a good-
looking, well-dressed, younger woman, is at the bar waiting for her boy
friend, PAUL. She is fidgeting with some (non-alcoholic) pink drink and
fixing her face. OLLIE enters wearing a mothballed suit, far out of style, tie
and hat. He looks around and spies NIKI. He inhales her fragrance. Then,
as if re-encountering some far-off memory, OLLIE arranges himself on the
barstool nearest to NIKI. NIKI glances OLLIE's way in the mirror.

OLLIE: (nods, tips hat into mirror)

NIKI: (continues applying cosmetics)

OLLIE: My, this is a nice hotel. That's a beautiful mirror. You can sit and watch everyone. Well, what's good here?
>(peers at her drink)
What are you having?

NIKI : (leaning forward into mirror) I'm waiting for my boyfriend.

OLLIE: You must like him a lot! You got here early!
>(NIKI gives OLLIE a dark look.)
I remember when my wife was still alive! I used to show up before my wife would arrive just because, ...I liked to watch her walk across the room! She could turn heads, let me tell you!
>(OLLIE mulls this for a while.)
You see, I have an ARTISTIC nature.
Yes, that feels about right. And I NEED to be around beauty in order to feel ALIVE. (to NIKI) So you see, I was walking past, and saw your lovely vision...
>(a beat)
If you are not 'artistic' by nature, this can be hard to understand.

NIKI: (truculent) I'm artistic.

OLLIE: (quickly) Oh? How so?

NIKI: I don't know. I just AM. Okay?

>(a beat)

OLLIE: Let me guess. Are you a... model?

NIKI: No.

OLLIE: An actress?

NIKI: No.

OLLIE: (admiring her breasts) You have lovely posture.

>(NIKI pulls her elbows in around her breasts.)

2

OLLIE: A bookish writer, then!

NIKI: No!

OLLIE: Well, what ARE you?

(a long beat)

NIKI: I sell cosmetics! Actually, I MANAGE the cosmetics department for a large department store. So you don't have to tell me about beauty. I make women beautiful everyday – for a living!

OLLIE: My hat is off to you!
(removing his hat, and placing it on the bar, making himself at home)
You are a professional. So you can understand my need to be here.
(OLLIE looking around nervously.)
Even to chat you up a bit, if I might?

NIKI: He's late!

OLLIE: (relaxing) Oh.

NIKI: Late! Late, as in… could be here at any moment, LATE! You got it?

(NIKI purses her lips, reaches in her purse and pulls out lipstick and applies it.)

(OLLIE gazes at her in the mirror.)

OLLIE: (leaning on his hand admiring her) You can tell a lot about women by the way they apply their cosmetics.

NIKI: (sticks out her tongue)

OLLIE: Some apply lipstick as if readying themselves for war, like a serious man putting on a tie.

NIKI : (shows her teeth)

OLLIE: Others apply cosmetics as if they were arranging furniture –
gauging just how it would divide the space, or create the effect they want.

> (NIKI finishes rolling her lips in on each other and judging her look
> in the mirror)

OLLIE: You apply lipstick as if you were mating with a peach. It's
incredibly arousing!

> (NIKI snaps her cosmetics case shut)

NIKI: (into the mirror) Paul didn't send you here, did he? That's just the
sort of practical joke he'd try.

OLLIE: No. I can't say I've had the pleasure of meeting this… (looking
around) Paul? Always thought I wouldn't fear anything when I got older.
But, in fact, as you get older you begin to fear everything! That crack in the
sidewalk? Is it worth the risk, or maybe you should go around? Maybe just
head back home.
> (a beat)
But! A HARVARD BUSINESS CONSULTANT once said that to find
success, "You need to know who you are when you're at your best."

NIKI: (doesn't answer)

OLLIE (squaring his shoulders) So myself, I'm at my best when telling
women how beautiful they are - when I'm in love! That's about all I'm good
for, really. To find love! To reveal beauty! To sniff it out like a truffle pig!
So here I am, staring into the lovely face of physical impairment or possibly
even death…
> (smiles at NIKI)
Perhaps you are at your best sitting in a bar with a lovely air of melancholy?
Or, even overt hostility! I know I was immediately riveted.
> (patting her hand)
We are all enthralled with success.
My guess is that your boyfriend's being late has nothing to do with you at all!

NIKI: Thanks.

OLLIE: My guess is that your boyfriend is out there doing whatever HE is best at... Crime – or possibly business? Am I right?

NIKI: (shrugs)

OLLIE: Well it's hard to get across to criminals OR business people the importance of beauty.
            (nods)
They're not much taken with cosmetics or little round mirrors either.

NIKI: (turning) True! He says to me all the time, "All your customers do all day is to look at themselves!"

OLLIE: And what do you say?

NIKI: "Maybe you should try it!"

OLLIE: That's a girl! "You need to create an environment around yourself." And then to defend it! That's another thing the Harvard business consultant on the public TV channel I watch, in the place I live, said.

NIKI: Paul has certainly accomplished that. I swear he has toadies coming out his ying-yang.

OLLIE: His what?

NIKI: (Points.)

OLLIE: Hmmm.

            (NIKI continues with her face.)

            (OLLIE gazes at her in the mirror.)

NIKI: People don't appreciate beauty. They don't appreciate how much time it takes; how much effort; how much expertise! They think it's something you can just gobble up... like a potato chip. Do you realize how much work it is to be me?

OLLIE: (leaning on his hand admiring her) It appears effortless.

NIKI: No. Being you is effortless. Have you ever taken a REALLY good look at your skin and nails? Had your pores done?

OLLIE: (takes a look at his pores) Uhh, no.

NIKI: Being me… Just for example, take these shoes. Aside from the hideous cost – these pumps are Prada, retailing at $495. That's just to get here. And what about hosiery? …nylons? You know anything about that?

OLLIE: Not a lot about nylons.

NIKI: I didn't think so. For example, when we talk about women's nylons we're talking 30 grades of sheerness based on the 'denier' index…

OLLIE: I'd just like to interject! that my "wandering around" in order to "seek out beauty" isn't the day at the beach it's cracked up to be, either, …especially at my age, when just getting out is like a jailbreak…

NIKI
…and various panty styles…

(NIKI's speech about panty styles cause OLLIE to pause momentarily, then continue.)

NIKI: …from the Control to the Sheer-to-the-Waist top

(THEY speak simultaneously.)

| OLLIE: And then say, for example, I do find someone beautiful …but am unable to get a word in edgewise! | NIKI: …which is perfect for "high slit gowns, mini-skirts and when wearing with lingerie". |

(a beat)

OLLIE: It sounds as though you may be angling out of cosmetics and into managing the entire women's department!

NIKI: You have a problem with that?!

OLLIE: I was just about to place an order!

NIKI: You laugh, but male pantyhose are a niche market that in my estimation is sure to grow as more and more elderly men opt for more warmth, support, …or for reasons of incontinence.
(with a nod to OLLIE's crotch)

OLLIE: (looking down) I have pee spots?

(NIKI indicates this is true.)

OLLIE: I guess I could use a little womanly advice.

NIKI: That's right. So we sell them out of the men's department, in some secluded area with cigar smoke and pictures of yachts which white-haired, older salts are sailing.

OLLIE: But maybe in a more masculine color like green or blue?

NIKI: And we never call them "nylons".

OLLIE: I don't know about that. "Nylons" has a sort of 'metro sexual' challenge to it. How much are you thinking these would retail for?

NIKI: Too soon to say. But, I don't see why we can't be competitive with something comparable to the women's prices.

OLLIE: Oh no, no. I'd go VERY hi-end. At least on introduction. Women would never purchase nylons at THIS price. They'd laugh at you! But you get men's competitive juices flowing - and they'll literally jump at anything. What you want, is to make this something only that prideful man on the splendid yacht would wear – and women NEVER consider.

NIKI: That's brilliant.

     (Throughout all this they've gradually turned to face each other.)

NIKI: You have more on your mind than I'd thought.

OLLIE: Life is a cold call. Until you've one foot in the door, you're just another jerk.

NIKI: You know, it's too bad people like you are shut away in homes.

OLLIE: Yes. It feels right.

NIKI: We all need to contribute!

OLLIE: I'd have to say, it feels right.

NIKI: It IS right. Do you realize that in about (checks her watch) fifteen minutes – you have made me feel better about myself and my career – just by listening – than my boyfriend, Paul, has in our 11 months of living together?

OLLIE: This is something.

NIKI: Something? It's everything!
All Paul has accomplished in our eleven months of living together is to get me pregnant!

     (a beat)

NIKI: (stops putting on make-up) I can't believe I said that.

OLLIE: Why?

NIKI: It's so… personal.

OLLIE: True. …But we're friends!

     (NIKI working on her hair.)

NIKI: I haven't even told Paul!
        (a beat)
I must be flipping out.
        (She brushes her hair hysterically.)

OLLIE: Goodness, calm down. Here, let me order you a Sprite.

NIKI: It's a virgin cosmopolitan!

OLLIE: I was about to tell you - that I'd marry you in a minute!
        (waits for a "yes")
So, you see, you've already one foot on a rock. The rest is just making a
decision about which way to turn. Towards Paul – who has brought all this
down upon you. Or to someone who has, in… sixteen minutes… made you
feel better about yourself and your career than Paul has in ELEVEN months
of co-habitation?

NIKI: (looks at OLLIE, laughs, with an edge of hysteria)

OLLIE: (offering her a hankie) Did I ever tell you that my first wife's son
was not my own? Did it make a difference? I can honestly say, "No."

NIKI: Your "first" wife?

OLLIE: Did I say that?

        (quite a while passes)

OLLIE: (dancing eyebrows) Did I ever tell you I used to …Direct?

NIKI: You worked in Hollywood?

        (a beat)

OLLIE: (stretching out the other arm) Yes!
…I must have worked in Hollywood.
And do you know what was my undoing?

NIKI: (shakes her head)

(a beat, as OLLIE thinks)

OLLIE: Those starlets. Those gorgeous, young, nymphets! They were like catnip to me.
    (closing his grasp)

NIKI: I've read that they will do about anything to get ahead.

    (a beat)

OLLIE: Yes! ...That's SO TRUE. "They would do anything to get ahead!"
    (OLLIE, aglow and lost in his thoughts)

NIKI: We were discussing Paul. And my PREGNANCY...

OLLIE: Oh yes, this PAUL.
    (a beat)
We will get to HIM. But first, I think it's important that we research your own motivations.
    (a beat, as OLLIE dons the affect of a Director)
If I could give you the perfect world from Ollie. What would it be? What do you WANT?

(AUTHOR'S NOTE: The following monologue is about the unattractive, unbecoming, clumsy, gauche, unsightly, unseemly, unbefitting, maladroit, inept, quality of PLEADING... ☺ As the monologue continues, NIKI will gather more of these qualities about her – as if she were collecting lint on her clothes.)

NIKI: What do I WANT?
    (a long beat)
Every day I attend these women, and I can see it. That they are just a hair! away from being beautiful. Which is what they WANT! We are all walking around looking so ordinary, when , real beauty is just a smile and a little authenticity. And we all have that! We're all so CLOSE. And that's what I try to tell Paul – when he's home. That we're so CLOSE. .
But I can't get that across to Paul. I'm failing! Because, the more I TRY to make it happen – the more we start fighting. And the more I TRY to make it come together; the more it falls apart. Until I feel paralyzed.

(pushing her cosmetics bag aside)
Real beauty requires an AUDIENCE! So, I guess what all these women and
I WANT – is not to feel so desperate! Why won't the world let us feel
happy?! Just a little smile in return? Just a little help?

OLLIE: Alright....

NIKI: (catching her breath) No, there's more...

OLLIE: Okay.

NIKI: So. I want... I want PAUL to grant me just a little
acknowledgement. Just a little ATTENTION. So that I'd know I'm done.
Finished! A completed work. I mean, is that too much to ask?
  (NIKI regards OLLIE – and the mess she's become in giving us
  this insight.)
Boy, if I'd talked to Paul this way, he would've been "OUTTA HERE", like a
shot.
  (NIKI looks glum.)

OLLIE: (nods) Would you believe it that when I awoke this morning, I was
feeling a little glum?
  (NIKI returns to doing her make-up.)
And the first thing I noticed was the tree, stood there on the linoleum with
several of the wire branches still bent from where they'd stuffed it into the
box last year. Then I saw a present already there from my friend, Don.
  (NIKI lowers her head to look at her upper lids and OLLIE takes
  this as a nod.)
Don was like an old hen, and always worried that he couldn't get out to BUY
me anything. Till sometimes I could just scream: "Don! What IS there I
need, that I don't already have? We're here to die, for Chrissakes!"
Till, one Christmas Season, I noticed that a pair of my best socks were
missing. And when I opened my present from Don that year, there they
were - my favorite socks. And I hollered, "Don, I've been looking all over
for these!" I was so pissed!
But Don was so pleased! Don wasn't the brightest bulb on the tree.
So. Anyway, I awoke this morning "feeling glum" (nods) and looking over
the rump of this other old fahrt, and thought, "Why, on earth, am I alive?"
When I saw Don's present. So I said to myself, 'I'm alive here, to get up this
holiday morning and open that present which Don left. And you know

what?

      (OLLIE points to his shined shoes. Wipes his eyes.)
They fit just right!

      (a beat, as smiling OLLIE looks for her reaction - and gets none)
I guess it dawned on me finally, that Don wasn't so stupid. Because I walked right out of there, and here I am... "Living the Dream"!

      (the sound of NIKI digging in her cosmetics bag annoys OLLIE)
Did you hear any of what I just said?!

NIKI: (digging in her cosmetics bag) Sure. Why? What did you just say?

OLLIE: I was just going on about how all my memories of the good things in my life were so shopworn as to be beyond consideration...

      (OLLIE sighs.)
Basically, it was about how I'd imagined that all of the good women in this world were dead - when I happened in here and found a woman SO beautiful... she takes my breath away.

      (NIKIE laughs, and stops her digging in the cosmetics case.)

NIKI: You miss Don?

      (a beat)

OLLIE: Who?

NIKI: Don! Your friend! It must have been hard when he died.

      (a beat)

OLLIE: (stricken) Don died?

NIKI: You said so.

OLLIE: I did?

NIKI: Well, in as many words... just a bit ago!

OLLIE: (sadly) I suppose it must be then.

NIKI: (exasperated) You can't remember?

OLLIE: I'm not sure. I looked down and saw the shoes I was wearing, and a story occurred to me. But often times I think I've made something up only to find out its true. I mean, I AM wearing some awfully nice shoes, which DO fit very well. Explain that?

NIKI: (sadly) You've lost your memory... of Don.

OLLIE: I'm not sure.

NIKI: (exasperated) Well you've either lost Don, or you've lost your memory!

OLLIE: Sounds more accurate. You see, my memories seem to go off on their own. And when they come back... well, there's no telling where they've been, or who they've talked to... (indicating NIKI) you know?

(a long beat)

NIKI: I guess Christmas has me sort of 'glum', too. And it's started getting to Paul, I can tell. Because his eyes will move around. Paul doesn't like glum. His eyes move around. He seems to have trouble concentrating. He can't follow what I'm saying. (perking up) That's why I like sitting here in this bar. You can be glum in a bar.

OLLIE: (toasting) A pair of 'glum-drops'. That's us.

NIKI: I don't know why I'm glum, especially. I mean I'm pregnant – and about to burst with new life. And lots of single moms live successful lives, nowadays. I just find myself feeling that way.

OLLIE: (glumly) Because you're in LOVE.

NIKI: I suppose.

OLLIE: LOTS of people, who are glum, are in love.

NIKI: The shoes I'M wearing were made in Italy. You want to know why? It's because Paul bought me these when we were last there. I love Italy.

OLLIE: I hear it's a nice place. And the food is good.

NIKI: Well, you heard right. The food is wonderful! I had to be very careful, or I would have billowed out like a blimp. So, instead, I would drink these little demitasse's of coffee at the café tables while I watched all of the street life. And they dress very well! And they all like women, a lot! I think even Paul got a little jealous.
I would wear this scarf tied around my neck like Gina Lollobrigida? And I would order a 'gelato'. Have you ever had one of those?

OLLIE: (thinking)

(OLLIE doesn't know.)

NIKI: Believe me. Even you would remember it if you had. They're light, and cool, and refreshing. I was eating one in this piazza just off the main thoroughfare in Bologna with this little spoon. Young men on Vespas honked as they drove past. Older men would tip their hats as they walked by and say, "Bon journo!" The breeze played with my hair. It was a wonderful, sunlit day. When Paul showed up they stopped their waving and honking – which was fine. When you're interested in a guy, it's always better to have a couple others interested in you, even if they're Italians. Maybe especially, if they are Italians.

OLLIE: I can understand.

NIKI: A girl can't be too careful. A guy like Paul has lots of opportunities. So you can't let him think for a moment that you're on his string – you know what I mean?

OLLIE: Oh yes. I understand fully.

NIKI: Because a guy like Paul, can look around – and everyone smiles. You know what I mean? That's hard to compete with.

OLLIE: I can imagine.

NIKI: I mean, even adoring guys – and by that, I don't mean gay guys – but just his pals. They want to know what he thinks of this; what he thinks of that. It must be intoxicating being that popular.

OLLIE: I would suppose.

NIKI: What is it? That's what I'd like to know. Because if I knew what it was, then maybe I could compete with it?

OLLIE: Maybe he's just confident. You know confidence can be infectious.

NIKI: I wish it would infect me.

OLLIE: (idea!) Maybe what you're in love with isn't Paul, but his confidence?

NIKI: I HATE his confidence. It's like this huge, WALL between us. Where does it come from? What makes it thrive so? If I could figure that out, then maybe I could STRANGLE it, and we could make some progress.
          (a beat)
Boy, do I sound like a shrew or what?

OLLIE: Is that what Paul calls you?

NIKI: He doesn't have to. He just has to give me that look…

OLLIE: …of confidence…

NIKI (nodding) …and I boil. It's like nothing in the world has anything to offer… anything that can compare, with this 'thing' he just carries around inside himself.
          (a beat)
I suppose he has, 'charisma'.

OLLIE: Sounds like a bad case.

NIKI: The worst. I mean, the WORLD loves him – and I'm just me.

          (a long beat, as OLLIE examines NIKI)

OLLIE: Did I ever tell you that I used to… 'Direct'?

NIKI: Are you sure?

OLLIE: No. But doesn't it seem like I might have?

      (NIKI sighs.)

OLLIE: Yes! And when they – the actors - were stuck… you know, when they couldn't get somewhere the script needed for them to go, …I would say to them:
      (stretching out his arm)
"Imagine that you're there, already! Imagine that you have miraculously acquired those feelings. Now tell me how that came to be?
      (a beat)
Everybody thinks that the playwright is the author of the script. Actually he is just the rough carpenter. It is stories within stories; wheels within wheels …and nuance! Which is what the 'Director' and actors, supply!

NIKI: We were discussing Paul.

OLLIE: Oh yes, that fellow Paul. You're trying to land this fellow Paul.

      (NIKI motions for OLLIE to keep his voice down)

NIKI: I'm not trying to "land" him. He's not a fish.

OLLIE: (sighs) Well, what do you want to achieve in this drama? I'll help you to do it! This is what directors do.

      (a beat)

NIKI: You think you could get me married?

OLLIE: (thinking HE'd marry her in a minute!) I KNOW I could get you married.

NIKI: Okay.

OLLIE: Great! Then we move forward. (as director) So here we are as the script begins: You love Paul. You want to marry him. …But he does not want to marry you.

NIKI: Why do you say that?!

OLLIE: Without it there's no story. There's no reason for us to be talking here.

NIKI: Alright. Fine. It just makes me nervous is all.

OLLIE: Which is all to the good. That's exactly the way you should feel! You are sitting here, in this bar. It's a fairly nice place! But you are early, and your fiancé is late. And he's been arriving later and later, more and more often. And it's got you worried. You've put your heart and your soul into this marriage.

NIKI: We haven't even discussed marriage.

OLLIE: All marriages are won or lost long before the discussion begins; that's a given. So what the playwright has done in this case is to simply cut to the chase. It raises the stakes, and gets us into the game.

NIKI: Fine. But it still makes me nervous.

OLLIE: All to the good.
        (rubbing his hands together excitedly)
So. We're in the first days of rehearsal and we're creating our first back-story: How did NIKI get PAUL to ask her to marry him? Once we know this, you can make your first entrance with confidence. You will know exactly where NIKI is coming from. So. Think back. How did this come about?

NIKI: I don't know. In fact, as time passes I'm having trouble even conceiving of it.

OLLIE: Okay. That's too big a bite. Let's take it one step at a time. How did your character… let's call her LORIE… feel when PAUL first asked you to marry him? If you can describe this to me, then we will know how you should first step onto that stage. Because this will describe the anticipation with which you are to meet him again.

NIKI: Okay. I feel – LORIE felt… wonderful. She felt as if her whole world suddenly made sense. She knew where she was; what she was; who she was, and where she was going next.

OLLIE: Wonderful! Now, you see, this is how you enter.

      (OLLIE indicates that she should leave, and then enter properly.)

      (Which NIKI does with erect, proud carriage of a future bride
      walking down the aisle.)

NIKI: (humming bridal entrance)

OLLIE: My God, that's wonderful.

      (OLLIE rises to take her arm, proudly.)

      (OLLIE seats a happy NIKI.)

OLLIE: But as you are sitting here, and PAUL's arrival looms later and later,
this whole wonderful creation is beginning to crumble.
      (NIKI, who has seated herself with 'class', slowly lets her
      composure crumble into 'pathetic'.)

NIKI: It felt so SOLID.

OLLIE: Yes! That was the whole point.

NIKI: And now it's feeling more and more like a sandcastle, as it is being
eaten away by my rising emotions!

OLLIE: I couldn't have put it better!

NIKI: (glowing with desperation) I can really feel Lorrie's dilemma.

      (NIKI looks up to see PAUL, who has just entered.)

OLLIE: Well. Here you must be!

      (PAUL stares at OLLIE with "Do I know you?" look.)

PAUL: Hey Niki. Sorry I'm late.

(a long beat, as PAUL tries to understand the scene)
You ready?

NIKI: We just got drinks.

PAUL: We're running twenty minutes behind as it is.

NIKI: That's because you're twenty minutes late.

(a beat)

PAUL: (laughing lightly) Alright. I'll buy.

NIKI: You already are.

(PAUL smiles back, nods.)

PAUL: (setting down money) Okay. There. Now everything's sweet.
Ready?

(OLLIE counting the money)

OLLIE: (to NIKI) ?! There's enough here for SEVERAL more drinks…

PAUL: (taking money back) That included the tip.

OLLIE: Oh, that's way too much. We should ALL have another.

PAUL: C'mon honey. (indicating OLLIE) Life is too short.

OLLIE: He's right! Shouldn't waste a minute of it with the wrong man.

NIKI: Isn't he the most unusual person?

(a long beat, as NIKI evaluates their mutual hostility)

NIKI: If you men will excuse me, I need to freshen up.

(OLLIE rises, as NIKI rises to leave.)
(PAUL doesn't rise; then rises at NIKI's glance.)

(NIKI leaves.)
(BOTH men sit.)

(a beat as the two men stare at each other)

PAUL: So. You're...?

OLLIE: (sticking out his hand again) Ollie. Ollie Brownstone.

PAUL: (shakes OLLIE'S hand) Paul. Paul Rasmussen.
So what brings you here, Ollie?
(smiles, taking in his outfit)
Besides ...romance?
(bearing down a bit with his handshake)
I would've thought you'd be retired by now?

OLLIE: (bearing back with his handshake) But what do you know? Huh.

(THEY break their handshake.)

OLLIE: Are you married?

PAUL: To Niki?

OLLIE: In general.

PAUL: No. I'm not generally married.

OLLIE: How about specifically?

PAUL: Nope.

OLLIE: Looks like you and I are natural adversaries then.

PAUL: You give yourself a lot of credit. When's curfew? (checking his watch) When do they want you back inside?

OLLIE: Oh, I'm free on my own recognizance.

PAUL: That's about as free as a soul could get, I'd imagine.

OLLIE: It's bracing!

PAUL: I bet.
          (Looks around. NIKI still hasn't come back.)
So, tell me. Just what DOES the world look like to a man like you?

OLLIE: You mean someone of my experience and latitude?

PAUL: I was thinking someone of your age. What with the sight and
hearing grow dim.   And your thoughts! just some tangle you haven't the
energy to consider.
          (looking OLLIE over)
Let alone clipping your ear hair or nails? When, what you'd REALLY like is
to take a long pee - followed by a good, satisfying, crap.

OLLIE: You, probably, should just keep your mouth shut - while we talk.
          (a beat)
Good. So first off, I think that it is best you know that...
          (straightening himself)
I love Niki.

PAUL: You love her? You just met her?

OLLIE: You don't believe in love at first sight?

PAUL: I believe in lust at first sight. I believe in 'infatuation' at first sight.
And I believe senility can strike well into your 70s – or even earlier!

OLLIE: Nope. This is love.

          (PAUL finding himself interested, and standing as if his hand were
          on the witness box railing)

PAUL: How do you know? How are YOU so certain?

OLLIE: (leaning forward, testifying earnestly) I'm 84. Believe me, I know.
And if you were 84, and a girl like NIKI spoke to you, believe me, you'd
know.
          (a beat)

21

You see, you're jaded from bumping too many available women. That's what's wrong with you. You, my boy, are a bit of a rake.

PAUL: (momentarily embarrassed in front of the jury)
I think to love someone, takes time – AND experience. Otherwise, how can you be sure? Why, it could just be a diminishment of blood flow to the brain.

OLLIE: So, you're the rational person here, all pinked up and with a great flow of blood to the brain. So. Tell me, Mr. Love Meister. How long exactly does love take?

PAUL: It takes long enough to know the person!
        (a beat)
What if you only THINK you love Niki - when all along it was just her breasts?

OLLIE: They're nice, aren't they? The fragrance of... (happy to have recalled it) gardenias!

PAUL: They're fine! But what are you going to do if one day you wake up! and realize that you and Niki, say, have 'nothing in common'?

OLLIE: What man ever had anything in common with a woman? Son, they're a complete mystery! Where have you been?

PAUL: Okay. But say you awake – to this "complete mystery" - and find it, SNORING.

OLLIE: I'd say, I'm glad I slept through it. What's more I'm glad just to wake up! and to greet another day! ...in the BED of a beautiful woman...

        (moves fast)

PAUL: She never cleans the house.

OLLIE: I can pick up after myself.

PAUL: She's a Democrat and you're a Republican.

22

OLLIE: Sounds like great sex.

PAUL: You try to talk to her about what is most important to you, like your job, or your hobbies - and she's busy watching Oprah!

OLLIE: (nodding) Sounds like lots of time to pursue your other interests.

PAUL: ...all the while covered in women's magazines. AND she spends money like it was water!

OLLIE: Turn off the tap.

    (a beat)

PAUL: (drilling in) She denies you sex.

OLLIE: This is serious. What would cause her to do that?

PAUL: This is just a hypothetical.

OLLIE: Okay. Hypothetically, what would cause her to do that?

PAUL: I don't know.

    (NIKI enters. PAUL doesn't see her.)

PAUL: Maybe she wants to get married?

OLLIE: I would marry her in a minute!

NIKI: (walking over to OLLIE) How are you, Ollie, my pet?

OLLIE: !! (purring) Your slave, my dear. Your absolute slave!

NIKI: (to PAUL) Isn't it nice that Ollie happened by?

    (lights down)

SCENE 2

SETTING: Lights up on the same, some time later. OLLIE and NIKI are chowing down on the bar snacks. PAUL is disgusted by it.

OLLIE: In a way, losing my memory was a blessing: a relief from those depressing, awful, bedeviling thoughts which used to haunt me – my days and nights – and intrude themselves upon every happy notion or positive development. Or, so I imagine. Anyway, I've reconciled myself to just making things up. It's not so bad. For example, (happy) I feel like we've just met!

PAUL: We have.

OLLIE: Did I tell you that for a long while I was actually worried about my WIFE's memory? That she couldn't remember a thing of what I had talked about?

PAUL: (urging NIKI to leave) Here's where we came in.

NIKI: (fascinated) So, you must live "entirely in the present"?

OLLIE: Yes. "Entirely in the moment."

PAUL: (to NIKI) Yes. And it's the SAME moment, over and over, again and again....

OLLIE: True. But, if you like where you are...
          (adoring NIKI)
...Why leave?

NIKI: (nibbling the bar food) Don't you like where you are, Paul?

(tearing his eyes away from NIKI' nibbling)

PAUL: (to OLLIE) You know, I have the feeling that I should hire you. That you would be very good in… some capacity…

OLLIE: Well, I'm certainly open to a position. We can talk.

NIKI: Paul! I'm a head-hunter! That's what I am. I can help you find people for your company.

PAUL: I was joking, Niki.

NIKI: Yes, but you were half-serious. Weren't you? Aren't you always saying about how you are looking for people who can think outside of the box?

PAUL: Yes, but not while living in one. There is a difference Niki between someone who has useful corporate ideas, and someone who has (announcing) "just left the grounds".

NIKI: You live in such an insular world. You know, you look like you do, but you don't.

PAUL: "Don't", what?

NIKI: Give people a chance.

PAUL: "Give people a chance?" A chance, at what?

NIKI: Demonstrating their value, their worth!
(a beat)
You just sweep through your world without a care. And you smile at this person, or decide to listen to that person and you are always very glib and friendly. But, you know, it's always because you've already settled the game long before. You've figured the game long before you ever entered the room, and so it's just a matter of accepting the accolades graciously as you sweep through to where you're next headed, like some little prince.

PAUL: Niki?

NIKI: You're just "phoning it in" Paul. You're not committed.

PAUL: I'm not committed? Honey, we are just going out to dinner.

NIKI: Tell me one thing you're absolutely committed to.

PAUL: Committed? Niki, if it's commitments you're interested in, then you came to the right person. Because I've got a THOUSAND commitments. That's what I'm continually trying to get across to you. Business is nothing if it's not a thousand different commitments, all of which have to be met or the whole structure – your whole credibility collapses. Which is why…
        (looking at his watch)
we were supposed to be at the Munson's "Feast for the Equinox" an HOUR and a HALF ago.

NIKI: (voice rising) Name something, that if you…

PAUL: Niki, honey, we're in a hotel bar.

NIKI: (crying) … imagined it missing would make you feel as if your every thought were just one more emotion eating away at the foundation of all that you relied upon?

PAUL: Huh?

NIKI: (bawling, getting sentimental) Is there ANYTHING that would get you really upset?!

PAUL: (taking her aside) Well. I guess that if my mother died…

NIKI: Paul. Your mother is fine!

PAUL: Then why are we… YOU… shouting?
        (a beat)
For a minute I thought you knew something about my mother that I didn't. But now it seems you are getting us back into the same argument we always have - though I haven't figured out quite what it is - in which you start

shouting for no reason!

NIKI: No one shouts for no reason!

(OLLIE waves for their attention.)

PAUL: (raising a finger) Often in a public place.

NIKI: Because you are a public person! I would LOVE to shout at you back in our apartment – but you're never there!

PAUL: ? (Notices OLLIE waving his hand.) What IS it?

OLLIE: I don't want to miss anything, or make you think that I'm leaving for any reason, because actually I'm quite interested.

PAUL: WHAT?

OLLIE: But …(to NIKI) Need to tiddle!

PAUL & NIKI: Go. Go!

(OLLIE waddles off to the restroom.)

(PAUL and NIKI continue to glare at each other.)

SCENE 3

SETTING: Same, later, as lights come up on OLLIE and NIKI talking. PAUL is missing.

NIKI: So, we had this big FIGHT and Paul says, "Niki you completely exasperate me." (looking around) And apparently left!

OLLIE: Perhaps a more mature man is what you need?

NIKI: But I'm young!

OLLIE: All the more reason. Two young people – put them together, and my God – it's like the blind leading the blind.
What you need is the benefit of some sage advice.

NIKI: I'm listening.

OLLIE: Marry me!

NIKI: Ollie. That's a wonderful offer. And I'm sure you would be very happy. But my heart is set on Paul.

(NIKI looks up in surprise.)

(PAUL re-enters, closing cell phone)

PAUL: Well. THAT got them all chatting. "I stiffed the Munsons". That's all you hear within cell range.

OLLIE: Word travels fast.

PAUL: "Word?" Whole sentences travel fast. Complete paragraphs travel even faster! I barely had a chance to get a word in edgewise, that "I did NOT stiff the Munsons". That I was just having an extended argument with my... Niki.

NIKI: You never call me that.

PAUL: Well, I could.

NIKI: (smiling) Yes, but you don't. I think you had something else in mind.

OLLIE: I know I OFTEN used to blame my tardiness on "arguments with my wife". It's such a natural thing to say that it was just accepted. Nobody would question me or try to pry into it.

PAUL: How would you know? You don't even have a memory.

OLLIE: That's true. But you've got to admit, it feels right.

PAUL: Yes. I suppose it does. It has that ring of naturalness to it. That's probably why it came to mind.

NIKI : To call me your "wife"?

PAUL: Only when we're arguing.

NIKI: But not otherwise?

PAUL: We're not married!

NIKI: I know!

PAUL: So why would I call you my wife?

NIKI: You tell me.

OLLIE: My, my, this has become very interesting.

NIKI & PAUL: You want to butt out?

OLLIE: Oh no, no.

PAUL: Then keep your mouth shut. Because my... NIKI and I are having a very important argument here.

NIKI: (with a glance to OLLIE) I don't know what about? Because I... under "no uncertain terms, and under no conditions would I ever, ever deign to marry YOU!"

OLLIE: (nods)

PAUL: (with a weaker voice) Why not?

     (NIKI looks to OLLIE)

OLLIE: (nods)

NIKI: Because... "The way I see it... I've.. tried ...him – and found YOU... lacking."

PAUL: (stares) Lacking???

     (a beat)

NIKI: "Lacking!" Because... well, the person I met was decisive and... "knew what they wanted". He said he loved me and took me to Italy! He made promises, and kept them! He was someone I KNEW I could depend on. He was a MAN. And now look at you.
     (a beat)
Why, you can't even keep an appointment with... the Munsons!

PAUL: ?

NIKI : AND... you're so BLIND. You think the world revolves around these people! And you can't even see why they're all after you! You spend so much of your time putting "up a front" – you can't even see that they're all clamoring for the fellow behind it – who has a GENIUS for numbers and can invariably spot an opening, a business opportunity. YOU know how to make money! Not THEM. YOU know how to put together a deal – not them. And yet you spend all of your time smoozing those stupid Munsons!

> (NIKI drops PAUL's cell phone into the water pitcher.)

And being late for the one person who is cheering you on.

> (PAUL rescues his phone and dries it off. It doesn't work, of course.)

PAUL: Okay! But why don't we try looking at things from my point of view? I'm in love with a woman who I have to look at in a mirror – because she's never looking anywhere else!

NIKI: (turning away from the bar mirror) In love?
> (a beat)

Where else is there to look? You're always gone.

PAUL: (ignoring this) And while we're at it: why in the world! are you eating like a PIG, lately?

NIKI: Because I'm pregnant!

> (PAUL looks at OLLIE.)

> (OLLIE raises his hands, innocently.)

NIKI: And I get hungry, okay?

> (NIKI, suddenly nauseous, covers her mouth.)

> (NIKI leaves hurriedly for the restroom.)

> (a long beat, as PAUL and OLLIE mull their drinks.)

PAUL: What a mess! I wish I could say it was all YOUR fault.

OLLIE: Me too!

PAUL: (gives OLLIE a dark look) Just SHUT UP, for a while. Okay?

OLLIE: (zips his lips)

>   (PAUL nods, sips his drink.)

>   (OLLIE sips his drink.)

OLLIE: Did I ever tell you that I used to direct?

PAUL: (slamming his drink) For Pete's sake!

OLLIE: I guess I must have.
>   (a beat)
Anyway, this all reminds me of something I used to tell my actors when we would finally reach that 'impasse', which ALL plays present. "THIS is why we are here," I would tell them. "THIS is why we practice our profession." And, "THIS is exactly where we want to be." "And you want to know why?"

PAUL: No!

OLLIE: Well, I'll tell you anyway. It's because right here, and right now, is where the CREATIVE mind takes over.

PAUL: (waves his hand) Go ahead. Take over.

OLLIE: Any knucklehead can go out there and get himself in a jam. Any bozo can go out there and knock a girl up and then abandon her. In fact, the world is OVERFLOWING with just these sorts of people. "Their name is legion." They often go by the name of, "just another screw-up."

PAUL: (hoisting his drink) Hello to you, too.

OLLIE: And I would go on to tell my assembled actors, "We are here to hoist the CREATIVE solution into view. We have already done the easy part: we have lived, or rather raped, life. Now is when we earn our money. This is where we give the audience something 'new and different'; something

they can take home with them and mull over.
>   (a beat)
In short, some NEW way of examining society and how it MIGHT operate, in a BRAVER and more DARING world!"

PAUL: I'm all ears. What do you propose?

OLLIE: I shall marry the girl!
>   (a beat)
You've got to admit: it's new; it's fresh; it's untried, and open to possibilities! What do you think? I'd like your okay, if possible. I think that might go a long way with her.

PAUL: (really dark look) No. frigging. way.

>   (PAUL takes a stiff drink and stares ahead.)

>   (a long beat)

>   (OLLIE sips his drink.)

OLLIE: Here's a thought!
>   (a beat)
How much of the success in our lives do you think is due to doing things we don't want to do?

PAUL: Probably none.

OLLIE: But it's an interesting question, don't you think?

PAUL: No.

>   (a beat)

OLLIE: You know, it's a wonderful treat getting to talk to you at this stage in your development.
>   (PAUL gives OLLIE a dark look.)
Because there is so much to talk about... to consider.

>   (PAUL indicates OLLIE needs to 'zip' his lip.)

OLLIE: (nods) Why do you think she's taking so long?

PAUL: I don't know "Mr. Director"... with all the answers. Could be a lot of reasons.
      (picks up on OLLIE's anxious concern)
(slyly) Maybe she left?

OLLIE: (face falls) Left?

PAUL: (seeing this) Sure! Sometimes she'll just take off – for no apparent reason.

OLLIE: I don't see why she would have done that.

PAUL: That's what "no apparent reason" means.

OLLIE: We were getting fairly close. We were getting along well, I thought.

PAUL: Well, that's how it goes.

OLLIE: You don't believe me, do you?

PAUL: Look pal, Niki has been known to talk to guys in bars. She likes conversation. She likes the mirrors. She likes to smoke – till they stopped allowing that. And then, she'll just disappear. Or not. For an old unflappable guy, who once was a Hollywood Director, you look kind of uncertain.

OLLIE: (shaken) I thought we'd made... a connection.

PAUL: I thought you knew something about women?

OLLIE: I thought I did. I mean, ...it felt right.

PAUL: Niki always 'feels right'. That's why we're cooling our heels. To tell the truth, we should BOTH probably head off to the Munsons. They have real money, and they throw a gala.
But then, on the other hand, there's Niki.

OLLIE: She had me riveted.

PAUL: What a jewel.

OLLIE: So you really like her?

PAUL: Of course. Why wouldn't I like her? Everybody loves Niki.

OLLIE: Everybody?

PAUL: You think it's coincidence you happened to bump in to her in a bar? I thought it was coincidence I happened to bump into her in a bar! Niki knows bars. It's just hard to get her out of one.

OLLIE: You know, I get a different story out of you, than I do from Niki.

PAUL: What a surprise.

       (a long beat)

OLLIE: You know, I have to pee again. I think I'll just go check on her.

       (PAUL bids him adieu.)

       (OLLIE shuffles towards the restrooms, just as NIKI is returning.)

OLLIE: !!! You came back!
       (OLLIE impulsively hugs her.)
Don't go away! …Just have to tiddle!

       (OLLIE exits, shuffling quickly.)

       (NIKI sits down next to PAUL.)

PAUL: (softly) Remember when we took that trip to Italy?

NIKI: All the time.

PAUL: What happened?

NIKI: I don't know! I was just telling Ollie about how wonderful Bologna felt! What with the early morning sun on all those colored café tables, and the breeze blowing, and all of the friendly pedestrians passing by.

PAUL: (remembering fondly) ...And you strolling the Plaza Neptune, dipping your fingers in the fountain.

NIKI: ?

PAUL: Poking your head into the shops. And speaking with that old gypsy-looking crone! You were almost skipping, afterwards. I had always meant to ask you about that?

NIKI: You said you had to go to the horse races!

PAUL: Yes, but then I got curious about how you spent your day.
          (a beat)
So then, as I followed, I realized how wonderful it was to follow a beautiful woman through an Italian town! It's like walking through a de Chirico – you know that Italian Surrealist painter?

NIKI: You were jealous... You were snooping on me!

PAUL: No. Just watching what you'd do. Italian men like you! It's as if you were sucking them in as you strolled. And I have to say, you know how to wander! And it got me thinking: Yours is a life that is easily absorbed. It's so easy to challenge: "Where are you going? What are you doing? What's that for?" What can you say? "I don't know?"
          All the while, I declare: "I'M going to the horse races, in order to bet." And there I go!
          I guess I realized how ALIVE you are - when I'm not around.

          (a beat)

NIKI: (suffers an epiphany) But you WERE around!
          (a beat)
Don't you see, Paul? It's just become clear now, why that day wandering around by myself went so well!
          (excited)
We created a vacuum!

36

PAUL: Niki, now don't get all wound up.

NIKI: Just follow me on this, Paul...
As you know, I like these holes in the day; these odd times with nothing in them – like mid-afternoons in bars - and these relationships – like ours! – in which we have NOTHING in common.

PAUL: I wouldn't go as far as to say that.

NIKI: (with the aggressiveness of hypomania) Just zip it!
(smiling) ...Okay?

PAUL: (nods)

NIKI: First we had nothing in common. And NOW we have something in common, for sure. JUST the sort of thing, which we can discuss. Some real, matter-of-fact, demanding, growing, infant-to-be! Which you are going to get to ask me all SORTS of very realistic, matter-of-fact questions and share concerns about.

PAUL: (starts to speak)

NIKI: (puts finger to her lips, silencing PAUL)

NIKI: Can you imagine any more certain way to be bound together? Even marriage pales besides THIS! ...sharing a baby!
        (epiphany keeps expanding)
We really needn't work so hard at ANYTHING, Paul – except getting rid of all the stuff we don't want or really need...

PAUL: (starts to speak)

NIKI: (silencing PAUL and continuing) You don't have to go to all the work of 'knowing' me; and I don't have to go to all the work of 'understanding' you... Because Nature will do all the work of replenishing that space. It has already filled my womb! "Nature abhors a vacuum," Paul! This is what is going on! ...on a COSMIC PLANE.

        (OLLIE enters, anxiously.)

37

(NIKI indicates that PAUL can now "speak".)

(PAUL is looking at NIKI as if she's lost it, and he can't think of anything to say)

OLLIE: (looking them over) Okay. I give. What have I missed?

(a beat)

PAUL: I'm not sure.

THE END

ABOUT THE AUTHOR

Carl Nelson spent 20 years in the Seattle theater community, during which time he wrote and produced plays, directed others, and performed whenever the talent was missing but a body still needed. Before that he did stand-up comedy. Currently he is enjoying the obscurity of Belpre, Ohio, where he writes poems that mosey about.